THE FOUNTAIN OF YOUTH --
GUARANTEED GRACE

John Coyle

Originally published 2013
Revised and expanded edition 2026

Printed in the United States of America

DEDICATION

Thank you, dear God,
for Your love,
for my children, grandchildren, and
great-grandchildren, and for Brooklyn, who
encouraged me to give this book new life.
Thank you, Bible Study Fellowship.

"Before I formed you in the womb I knew you, before you were born I set you apart; I appointed you as a prophet to the nations."—Jeremiah 1:5

For every child born into this world—
may you discover early what took humanity millennia to find: the Fountain of Youth that flows freely through Jesus Christ.

And for every child in every nation—
known by God before birth and loved beyond measure—may you find this gift before the world tells you it doesn't exist.

"For you created my inmost being; you knit me together in my mother's womb."—Psalm 139:13

TETELESTAI

"It Is Finished" – Paid In Full

There is a word so complete, so final, that when Jesus Christ spoke it from the cross, nothing more could be added and nothing could ever be taken away.

The veil would soon be torn in two from top to bottom—declaring that the debt had been satisfied in full.

Tetelestai.

In the ancient world, this word was written across a debt when it had been fully paid.

The balance was zero.
The account was closed.

It could never be reopened or charged again.

When Jesus spoke this in the midst of His suffering, while hanging on the cross, He was not announcing an end—

He was declaring completion.
The work was done.
The payment was made.

The matter was forever settled.

And within this same word is the quiet perfection of a finished work—exactly as it was meant to be.

Nothing left undone.
Nothing left outstanding.

Tetelestai means the striving can stop, because nothing more will ever be required.

The answer has already been given.
The work stands complete.

This is the word that settles everything before the first chapter even begins:

The account is closed.
The balance is zero.

And what is finished remains finished forever.

It is enough.
You are free.

INTRODUCTION
THE FOUNTAIN OF YOUTH – GUARANTEED GRACE

The Longing That Never Leaves

There is a longing inside every human heart that never fully goes away. It doesn't matter where you were born, what language you speak, what century you live in, or what you believe. Rich or poor, young or old, educated or unschooled—every person feels it.

It is the longing to belong.
The longing to be loved completely.
The longing for home.

We feel it in quiet moments when success feels hollow. We feel it in crowded rooms when loneliness still lingers. We feel it when we achieve everything we set out to accomplish—and yet something inside us whispers,
"Is this all there is?"
This longing is not a weakness. It is not a flaw.
It is not something to ignore or outgrow.
It was placed inside you by God Himself.

You were created with eternity in your heart. You were designed for something beyond this temporary world. And no matter how beautiful, successful, comfortable, or thrilling this life becomes—nothing here can fully satisfy what you were made for.

"He has made everything beautiful in its time. He has also set eternity in the human heart, yet no one can fathom what God has done from beginning to end."—Ecclesiastes 3:11

God planted eternity inside you. That is why nothing temporary ever feels like enough. That is why even your greatest joys are tinged with longing. That is why love, beauty, peace, and happiness in this world—as real as they are—always leave you wanting more. Because this world is not your home. **It never was.**

The Search Across History. For thousands of years, humanity has searched for something we could not fully name but could never stop chasing. We have called it many things:

- The Fountain of Youth
- Eternal life

- Immortality
- Paradise
- Nirvana
- Enlightenment
- The perfect life

What do you call it?

But beneath all these names, the search has always been the same: We want to live forever in a place where we are loved, where we belong, where nothing is lost, where pain ends, where decay stops, and where we are finally home.

Ancient explorers sailed across unknown oceans searching for mythical waters that could grant eternal youth. Kings and emperors poured fortunes into alchemists and physicians, hoping to discover the secret to immortality. Philosophers debated the nature of the soul, trying to reason their way into eternal meaning. Religions built elaborate systems of rituals, sacrifices, and disciplines—hoping that if they performed correctly, they might earn their way into eternal peace. And the search continues today. Modern science chases longevity through medicine, genetics, and technology. People spend billions on anti-aging treatments, fitness regimens, and wellness trends—hoping to slow time, preserve youth, and delay death. Others search through spirituality, meditation, self-help, and personal transformation—hoping to find inner peace and transcendence.

But here is the truth no one wants to hear: **None of it works.** Not because the efforts are insincere. Not because people are foolish. But because the thing we are searching for cannot be earned, discovered, purchased, or achieved. **It can only be received.**

What We've Lost in the Search

The cost of this endless search has been staggering. Billions of people across thousands of years have exhausted themselves climbing ladders that lead nowhere. They have performed endless rituals, hoping to earn favor from gods they feared.

They have fasted, sacrificed, and punished their bodies, believing suffering would make them worthy. They have built monuments and conquered nations, hoping their names would outlast death. They have chased beauty through surgeries and serums, only to watch time win anyway. They have pursued wealth, believing security could be bought only to discover that money cannot purchase peace.

They have sought knowledge until their minds grew weary—and still found no rest for their souls. They have worked themselves to collapse, believing that if they could just achieve enough, do enough, become enough—then perhaps they would finally feel whole.
But they never do.

The wealthy lie awake at night, anxious.
The powerful feel empty.
The beautiful grow older.
The brilliant still question their purpose.
The religious still fear they haven't done enough to be saved. And the world continues its cycle—generation after generation, searching, striving, failing, and passing away.

Why?
Because we have been searching in the wrong place. The answer has always been there.
Here is what humanity has missed for so long:
The Fountain of Youth is not hidden.

It has never been hidden. It is not buried in a distant land. It is not locked behind secret knowledge. It is not reserved for the elite, the enlightened, or the religiously perfect.

The Fountain of Youth is Heaven.
It is eternal life in the presence of the God who created you, loves you, and has been calling you home since the moment you were born.
It is not about becoming younger in body.

It is about becoming whole forever—body, soul, and spirit—in perfect love, peace, joy, and belonging with your true Father.

"You will show me the path of life, in Your presence is fullness of joy; At Your right hand are pleasures forevermore." —Psalm 16:11

This is not a myth. This is not wishful thinking. This is not religious fantasy designed to comfort the weak. This is the truth that has been confirmed across thousands of years through the Living Word of God, the testimony of millions of believers, and the unchanging character of the One who made this promise.

Heaven is real.
Eternal life is real.
The Fountain of Youth is real.

And the way to it is not a system, a ritual, or a lifetime of perfect performance. The way is a Person. Jesus Christ: The Door to the Fountain There is only one Door to the Fountain of Youth. Not many doors. Not multiple paths. **Not "whatever works for you."**

One Door.
One Way.
One Name: Jesus Christ.

Come close to God, and God will come close to you.—James 4:8

For there is one God and one mediator between God and mankind, the man Christ Jesus, who gave Himself as a ransom for all people.—1 Timothy 2:5-6

Jesus is not one option among many.
He is not a good teacher, a wise prophet, or an enlightened guide pointing you toward truth.

Jesus IS the Truth

He is the living revelation of God's love. He is the fulfillment of every promise God has ever made. He is the sacrifice that paid the price for every sin, every failure, every moment of separation between you and your Creator.
And He is the only way back home. This is not narrow-mindedness. This is not religious exclusivity. This is not arrogance.
This is mercy.

Because if there were any other way—any other path that could bring you to eternal life, heal your soul, and reconcile you to God—then Jesus would not have needed to die.
But He did die. And He rose again. And in doing so, He opened the Door that had been closed since humanity first turned away from God.

"For God so loved the world that he gave his one and only Son, that whoever believes in him shall not perish but have eternal life."
—John 3:16

This is the Gospel.
This is the Good News.

This is the love story that spans all of human history. **This Book Is Your Invitation.**
This book is not a history lesson. It is not a theological argument. It is not a set of rules or rituals you must follow to earn God's approval.

This book is an invitation. An invitation to stop searching and start receiving. An invitation to stop striving and start resting. An invitation to stop running and come home.

You have been searching for the Fountain of Youth your entire life—perhaps without even realizing it. Every time you felt that longing for something more. Every time success felt empty. Every time love felt incomplete. Every time you wondered, **"What is the point of all this?"**
That was your heart crying out for home.
And God has been answering that cry all along.

"You will seek me and find me when you seek me with all your heart."—Jeremiah 29:13

The Fountain of Youth you have been searching for is not far away. It is not complicated. It is not out of reach. It is right in front of you.

Heaven is real. Jesus Christ is the Door. And God is calling you home—not because you are perfect, but because He loves you.

What This Book Will Show You.

In the pages ahead, you will discover:

- Why every human heart longs for eternal life—and why nothing in this world can satisfy that longing.
- How God has been pursuing humanity for thousands of years—with patience, love, and grace.
- What it means that Jesus Christ is the Fountain of Youth—the way, the truth, and the life.
- How you can receive eternal life today—not by earning it, but by accepting the free gift God offers.

This is not complicated. This is not mysterious. This is not reserved for the religious elite.

This is simple, clear, and available to everyone.

The Fountain of Youth is Guaranteed—not by human promise, but by God Himself. And the invitation is open to you.

The Journey Begins.
What if the thing you have been searching for your entire life is not something you must achieve, earn, or become worthy of—but something already offered to you in love? What if the Fountain of Youth is not far away, hidden, or reserved for the few—but open, near, and calling your name? **What if you could stop striving and simply receive?**

This is the love story God has been writing since the beginning of time.

A story of a Father who will not give up on His children.

A story of perfect love reaching into a broken world. A story of the Door standing wide open —waiting for you to walk through.

BEFORE YOU MEASURE GOD BY MAN

Why Earthly Fathers Can Distort the Image of the True Father Before we go any further, something important must be said—especially for those whose experience with the word father carries pain, confusion, fear, or disappointment. Not every earthly father reflects love. Some abandon. Some wound. Some misuse authority. Some are absent, cruel, or even evil. If that has been your experience, you are not alone—and God is not offended by your hesitation.

Here is a truth that must be clear before your heart can safely receive what follows:

God the Father must never be measured by broken men. Human fathers—no matter how well-intentioned—are flawed and limited. Some fail through weakness. Others through selfishness or harm. And even the best earthly father who ever lived could only offer a faint and incomplete glimpse of what true fatherhood was meant to be.

This is why Jesus spoke these words:

"And do not call anyone on earth 'father,' for you have one Father, and he is in heaven."—Matthew 23:9

Jesus was not denying family relationships.

He was correcting spiritual confusion. He was drawing a clear boundary between human authority and divine Fatherhood—because when God is filtered through wounded human experience, the heart often closes before it even realizes why.

Some people hear "Father" and think:
- Control instead of care
- Judgment instead of mercy
- Conditional love instead of grace
- Anger instead of patience
- Absence instead of faithfulness

But that image does not come from God. It comes from men. God is not a larger version of an earthly father. He is not humanity magnified. He is authority without abuse, holiness without cruelty, power governed by love, and mercy without condition.

Even the strongest and kindest father on earth will eventually disappoint—because he is human. He grows tired. He makes mistakes. He ages. He dies.

But God does not weaken. God does not abandon. God does not fail. God does not change.

"Though my father and mother forsake me, the LORD will receive me."
—Psalm 27:10

This verse exists because God knows how deeply human fatherhood can fail—and how profoundly that failure can shape a heart.

If your earthly father distorted your understanding of love, God does not ask you to ignore that reality. He asks you to separate Him from the one who failed you.

God never abused authority. God never used fear to control. God never withheld love as punishment. When God reveals Himself as Father, He is not asking you to relive pain. **He is offering to heal it.**

This book is not asking you to trust men. It is not asking you to excuse what was done to you. It is asking you to meet a Father unlike any you have known. A Father whose love does not expire. A Father whose mercy is not earned. A Father who restores rather than wounds.

If the word father has been heavy for you, let this truth lighten it: God is not like any other father or the father who might have failed you. **And He never will be.** But who is this Father who has been calling you home across thousands of years? What kind of God loves humanity with such relentless pursuit—even when we turn away, even when we ignore Him, even when we wander in confusion?

To understand the invitation, you must first understand the One extending it. Let me show you the love affair that has defined all of human history.

CHAPTER 1
GOD'S UNLIMITED LOVE AFFAIR WITH MANKIND

The Perfectly Ordered Heavens and the Confused Heart

A God-Centered Chapter of Awe, Humility, and Love. Perfect order exists only because of our Creator and Father.

"He determines the number of the stars and calls them each by name."
—Psalm 147:4

The Holy Silence of the Heavens

If I took credit for this book, I would be lying. It would be no different than when Moses took credit for striking the rock and water came out. God told Moses to strike the rock, and God made the water come out. Moses was the instrument, **God was the source of power.**

God told me to write this book, and I am writing because God has blessed me with insight. To take credit would be to steal the truth and glory that belongs to Him alone.

"Unless the LORD builds the house, the builders labor in vain. Unless the LORD watches over the city, the guards stand watch in vain." —Psalm 127:1

Whatever truth exists in these pages flows from the mercy of a Father who opens minds and plants seeds of understanding.
The power was never in the pen.
The power is in the Word of the Lord.

There is a holy silence in the night sky that no city can fully drown out. Even in the loudest century of human history, when screens glow and engines roar and nations argue without pause, the heavens continue their quiet work.

The stars do not need permission to shine. The moon does not ask whether mankind approves of its path.

The sun does not debate its schedule.
Creation moves as though it knows something humanity keeps forgetting: there is a King above it all, and His Word does not tremble. The greatest tragedy is not that mankind lacks

information. The tragedy is that mankind has lost its wonder. And yet the greatest mercy is this: **God has not lost His love.**

If every mind on earth were gathered into one council, and every computer were linked into one vast network, we would still be like children standing at the edge of an ocean—unable to measure its depth, unable to name its boundaries, unable to see where it ends.

If every person on earth joined minds, and every computer processed data without rest, we would still look absolutely ignorant compared to the mighty power, love, grace, and superiority of our loving God. The power, wisdom, and love of God are not merely "greater than ours."

They are beyond our category of greater.

They are the difference between
The Creator and the created.

No one will ever know His power and His brilliance. He is Almighty and beyond perfection.

“He is Almighty—beyond all human understanding of perfection”

Not fully explained. Not reduced.
Not captured by language.
But known-personally-by Grace.
And still—this same God who cannot be comprehended has chosen to be known.
This chapter is not an argument against mankind. It is not an accusation thrown at wandering hearts. It is an invitation into awe.

It is a reminder that the One who made the galaxies is also the One who bends low to touch a bruised spirit. God's superiority is not cold.
It is tender. His holiness is not cruel.
It is radiant. His power is not violent.
It is governed by love. God is the focus. God's love is the focus. God's grace is the focus. God's majesty is the focus. And mankind—mankind is the mystery God refuses to abandon.

1. **The Heavens: Perfect Order That Does Not Explain — It Points**

The heavens move without hesitation. The sun rises and sets on a schedule it did not choose.

The moon pulls the tides as it has since the beginning. Seasons arrive and depart in their appointed time. The Earth turns minute by minute—never drifting too close to the fire that would consume it, never slipping too far into cold that would destroy it. It rests where it was placed—sustained, protected, restrained.

Nothing in creation appears confused about its purpose. **And yet humanity is.**

We were meant to recognize this order.
We were meant to feel the weight of it—not the weight of fear, but the weight of meaning.
The heavens are not a random painting.
They are a signature.

"The heavens declare the glory of God; the skies proclaim the work of his hands."—Psalm 19:1

Creation preaches without shouting.
It testifies without arguing. It stands as a daily witness that God is faithful, precise, and sovereign. And God is not merely powerful in a distant sense. **He is personal.**

He determines the number of the stars and calls them each by name. Mankind struggles to remember names in a crowded room.
God names what we cannot count.
He does not merely sustain the stars.
He knows them. If God calls them, they respond. If God wills, they remain.
If God commands, creation obeys.
This is the majesty of a Father who holds the universe without strain.

2. God Before Creation:
The One Who Needs Nothing

Before there were oceans, God was.
Before there was time, God was.
Before there were constellations, God was.
Before there were hearts to hunger, God was.
God is not a human being enlarged.
God is not the universe's highest creature.
God is not the sum of all intelligence.
God is the eternal **"I AM"**—the One who does not borrow existence from anything else.

"In the beginning God created the heavens and the earth."—Genesis 1:1

The beginning is not a place God discovered.

It is a point God started. When God speaks, reality answers. When God wills, matter forms. When God commands, light appears. And the wonder of it is not merely that He can do this. **The wonder is that He chooses to do it for a purpose that includes us.**

3. The Shocking Center: God's Superiority Is Wrapped in Grace

Here is what the wandering heart needs to hear, maybe more than any other truth:
God's greatness is not merely His power.
God's Greatness is His Grace.

If God were only superior, mankind would hide forever. If God were only powerful, mankind would tremble without hope. **But God's superiority is clothed in tenderness.** His authority is governed by love. His holiness is not a weapon; it is light. He does not lead His children like tyrants lead subjects. He does not coerce by brutality. He does not train hearts through terror. He does not offer Himself through domination. He offers Himself through dignity, patience, mercy, and the sacrifice of His own Son. That is a kind of greatness no human ruler has ever mastered.

Not just superiority—but Grace. God touched mankind. **God loves us and gives us favor.**

4. Mankind:
Spiritually Sick, and Still Loved
Every human being is spiritually challenged to a degree—some less, some more. This is not said with contempt. It is said with compassion. The sickness shows up as pride that refuses to kneel, fear that refuses to trust, desire that refuses to be satisfied, and a restless spirit that keeps searching for life in places that cannot give it. The sickness is not merely moral failure; it is separation—distance between the heart and the God it was designed to know.

We are the wanderers.
God is the way home. And yet, even in our sickness, God does not step away in disgust. **He steps closer in mercy.**

5. Why Does God Put Up With Us?
The Mystery of Love
If we are honest, the question rises in the heart: Why would God want anything to do with mankind? Mankind is capable of astonishing

cruelty. Mankind destroys what it claims to love.

**Mankind often worships itself,
then wonders why it feels empty.**

Mankind can be so self-seeking that it looks like a disease—spreading greed, violence, deception, and confusion from generation to generation. **And still God loves.**

No mind can comprehend why God loves us.

"God is love." —1 John 4:8

Not "God loves sometimes."
Not "God loves when we earn it."
God is love.

That is why He pursues what does not deserve pursuit. That is why He seeks what does not seek Him. That is why He keeps calling wandering hearts home.

6. Made in His Image: God Plants Seeds of Wisdom

"Then God said, 'Let us make mankind in our image, in our likeness...'" —Genesis 1:26

"So God created mankind in his own image... male and female he created them."—Genesis 1:27

To be made in God's image means humanity was designed differently than the rest of creation. **The stars obey without thought.** The animals follow instinct without choice. The Earth turns without awareness.

But mankind was given something unique: A mind that can seek wisdom. A will that can choose. A heart that can love. A spirit that can commune with the Creator. This is why the whole story of human history makes sense. This is why God plants seeds of knowledge in human minds.
We were made for this. God did not create us to remain ignorant. He created us with the capacity to learn, to think, to imagine, to build.

But here is the mercy woven into the design: God does not leave us to figure everything out alone. He guides. He reveals. He opens minds. He plants insight at the right time.

"Every good and perfect gift is from above, coming down from the Father of the heavenly lights..." —James 1:17

The world calls it Genius.
Heaven calls it Gift.

7. The Famous Men — and the Deeper Truth Behind Their Greatness

This is where we must be honest.
Many men have been called brilliant.
Many minds have changed the world.
Many discoveries have improved human life.
But no man created order. Men discover what God allows them to see. The laws were already there. The consistency was already there.
The intelligibility of the universe was already there. And that itself is a testimony:

Creation is structured because
it came from God, our loving Father.

Example One: Gutenberg and the Spread of the Written Word.
When Johannes Gutenberg's printing press accelerated the spread of knowledge, the world changed. Books could be reproduced faster than hand-copying. Literacy and learning grew. Ideas traveled. But a God-centered heart sees something deeper than mechanics.

Why did this happen in that era? Why did words gain wings? Why did knowledge begin to multiply? Because God was widening the field. Even when men did not intend to glorify God, God used the multiplying of the written word to bless humanity—and in many places, to spread Scripture itself. God is not limited by human motives. He can steer history with a steady hand, even through imperfect instruments.

Example Two: Leonardo da Vinci and the Gift of Imagination.
Leonardo da Vinci imagined machines long before the world was ready to build them. Sketches of flight. Designs beyond his century. The world calls it genius.
But what is genius, if not a spark of sight?
And what is sight, if not a gift?

A person cannot imagine what they cannot conceive. They cannot draft what their mind cannot picture. They cannot move beyond the assumptions of their age unless something opens inside of them. Where does that opening come from? From a Creator who made mankind in His image—creative, curious, visionary—and who still touches minds with glimpses of what is possible.

Example Three: Nikola Tesla and the Laws of Electricity.

When Nikola Tesla helped advance alternating current, cities could be lit. Industries could expand. Life was transformed. But Tesla did not create electricity. He did not author the laws that govern electrical flow. He discovered what already existed. And here is the deeper point: If creation were chaos, science would be impossible. If the universe were random, engineering would collapse. If the world were without order, there would be nothing to discover. The very possibility of scientific progress **testifies to prior divine order.**

Example Four: The Wright Brothers and the Laws of Flight.

When the Wright brothers achieved powered flight, the world crossed a threshold. But they did not invent air. They did not create lift. They did not design the principles that govern motion. They studied, tested, and refined—but the laws were already there. **Science works because God's world is consistent.** Engineering works because God's laws do not change with human opinion.

Example Five: Louis Pasteur and God's Mercy in Healing.

Louis Pasteur's work helped reduce suffering, prolong life, and protect families from avoidable death. And again, the deeper lens sees this: Healing aligns with God's heart. God does not delight in death. God does not celebrate suffering. God enters brokenness with mercy. Even when mankind does not give God recognition, God continues to allow discoveries that preserve life —**because Grace is not earned. It is given.**

8. The Tragedy of Forgotten Glory: Mankind Takes Credit Without Gratitude.

Here is the sorrow beneath history:
So many people receive life, insight, opportunity, and blessing—then act as if God had nothing to do with it. They celebrate their minds **while ignoring the One who gave them breath.** They take credit for "their" ideas while refusing to acknowledge the Source of intelligence.

"The wrath of God is being revealed from heaven against all the godlessness and wickedness of people, who suppress the truth by their wickedness... since what may be known about God is plain to them, because God has made it plain to them... For since the creation of the world God's invisible qualities—His eternal power and divine nature—have been clearly seen, being understood from what has been made, so that people are without excuse" —Romans 1:18–20

The problem has never been lack of evidence.
It has been the refusal of the heart.

Instead of humility, mankind chose autonomy.
Instead of gratitude, we chose control.
Instead of worship, we chose self-rule.
And in doing so, the human heart drifted into confusion while creation remained steadfast.
The Earth did not fall. Humanity did.

9. God's Strange Victory: He Conquers Without Cruelty.

God does not win the way the devil wins.
He does not rule the way tyrants rule.
He does not dominate the way empires dominate. **God traffics in truth,** mercy, conviction, restoration, and life. God is not fighting for mankind because mankind is strong. God fights for mankind because His love is strong. And then God does what no human mind could invent:
He humbles Himself.

10. The Unthinkable Humbling: God Comes Down.

The Creator entered His own creation. The One who named the stars came among the people who would reject Him. The One who set the moon in place walked under its light as a Man.

The One who sustains breath allowed His own breath to be mocked. This is not a loss of power. **This is power restrained by love.**

"He was in the world... and the world was made through him, and the world did not recognize him." —John 1:10

"But God demonstrates his own love for us in this: While we were still sinners, Christ died for us." —Romans 5:8

This is the center:
God did not offer salvation through force.
He offered salvation through sacrifice.
Jesus Christ is the greatest revelation of God's love affair with mankind.

11. The Fountain of Youth: Not Invention, But Reconciliation.

Mankind can advance in knowledge and still be starving. Mankind can invent machines and still be lost. Mankind can build cities and still feel alone. Mankind can conquer space and still not know peace.

Why?

Because the deepest hunger is not physical.
It is spiritual.

The Fountain of Youth is not found in technology or health hacks or human progress.

It is found in reconciliation with the Creator—through Jesus Christ.
This is the youth that does not age.
This is the life that does not fade.
This is the love that does not withdraw.

12. An Invitation to Wandering Hearts.
If you are tired—God sees you. If you are ashamed—God knows your name. If you are confused—**God is not confused.** If you have been wandering—God has been pursuing.
Look up at the heavens again.
They are perfectly ordered. They remain obedient to the God who made them.
They do not save us—but they point us to the One who can. And the wonder is this: The God who holds the stars is willing to hold you.

"Come to me, all you who are weary and burdened, and I will give you rest."
—Matthew 11:28

CHAPTER 2
THE LONGING GOD PLACED IN EVERY HEART

From the beginning of time, humanity has carried a deep, undeniable longing—a hunger for something beyond this life.

We sense there must be more than what we see and experience in our brief years on earth. This longing isn't accidental. God placed it within every human heart.

As the deer pants for streams of water, so my soul pants for you, my God. My soul thirsts for God, for the living God. When can I go and meet with God?
—Psalm 42:1–2

God designed us with an awareness of eternity. We instinctively know this life isn't all there is. Deep within, we long for permanence, for meaning that transcends our mortality.

The Universal Search:
Throughout history, people of every culture have sought immortality. Ancient civilizations

built monuments meant to last forever. Emperors searched for elixirs of eternal life. Philosophers pondered the nature of the soul. Even today, scientists pursue ways to extend human life indefinitely.

This universal search reveals a profound truth: we were made for eternity. The longing we feel isn't a cruel joke or evolutionary accident—it's God's signature within us, pointing us toward our true home.

The Emptiness That Drives Us

Without God, this longing creates a deep emptiness. We try to fill it with achievements, relationships, pleasures, and possessions. **Yet nothing fully satisfies.**

We climb the ladder of success only to find it's leaning against the wrong wall.

Jesus explained why so many hearts remain restless:

"Do not store up for yourselves treasures here on earth, where moths eat them and rust destroys them, and

where thieves break in and steal. But store up for yourselves treasures in heaven, where moths and rust do not destroy, and where thieves do not break in and steal. For where your treasure is, there your heart will be also."— —Matthew 6:19-21

Earth cannot satisfy an eternal soul. No amount of money, achievement, beauty, pleasure, or success can remove the homesickness within us. We were created for something greater than temporary possessions and the temporary years that we are given here.

Deep down, the human heart longs for permanence—for the eternal home that only God can provide.

"All things are wearisome, more than one can say. The eye never has enough of seeing, nor the ear its fill of hearing." —Ecclesiastes 1:8

No matter how much we acquire or accomplish, something remains missing.

That "something" is actually Someone—the God who created us for relationship with Him.

God's Intentional Design

God placed this longing within us intentionally. He wants us to seek Him, to recognize that only He can satisfy the deepest hunger of our souls.

"From one man he made all the nations, that they should inhabit the whole earth; and he marked out their appointed times in history and the boundaries of their lands. God did this so that they would seek him and perhaps reach out for him and find him, though he is not far from any one of us."—Acts 17:26-27

God isn't hiding from us. He's placed eternity in our hearts specifically so we would search for Him—and find Him.

The Longing Points Home.

This God-given longing is actually homesickness. We're yearning for the place we were designed to be—in perfect fellowship with our Creator, living in the eternal home He's prepared for us. Our longing for eternity, for permanence, for something beyond death—this isn't weakness. It's God's voice within us, calling us home to Him.

Now you understand the longing—the hunger that drives you, the homesickness that never leaves. But for thousands of years, humanity has tried to satisfy this longing through our own efforts.

Let's examine why every human attempt to reach heaven has failed—and why it had to fail.

CHAPTER 3
WHY HUMAN EFFORT CAN NEVER OPEN THE DOOR

Understanding our longing for eternity is one thing. Trying to reach it through our own efforts is another entirely. For thousands of years, humanity has attempted to bridge the gap between earth and heaven, between mortality and eternal life. Every attempt has failed, and there's a compassionate reason why.

The Great Cathedrals. For over 2,000 years, people have built magnificent structures reaching toward heaven. They made every effort to show their love and dedication and surround the **written Word of God and His Image.**

So they spent decades—sometimes generations—building magnificent structures out of love. The great cathedrals of Europe stand as testaments to human devotion and ambition. Generations of craftsmen spent their entire lives constructing these architectural marvels, hoping their efforts would somehow bring them closer to God. These buildings are

breathtaking. They inspire awe.
But they cannot save a single soul.

This is what the Lord says: "Heaven is my throne, and earth is my footstool. Where is the house you will build for me? Where will my resting place be? Has not my hand made all things, and so they came into being?" declares the Lord —Isaiah 66:1-2

No matter how beautiful or costly our constructions, they cannot earn us entrance into heaven.

The Sincere Search:
Good Works and Religious Rituals.
Throughout history, people have tried to reach God through:

- Performing religious ceremonies
- Following strict rules and regulations
- Making sacrifices and offerings
- Living morally upright lives
- Helping others and doing charitable works

These aren't bad things.
Many are good and beneficial.
Many come from sincere hearts seeking God.

But here's the compassionate truth:
they cannot purchase eternal life.

"All of us have become like one who is unclean, and all our righteous acts are like filthy rags; we all shrivel up like a leaf, and like the wind our sins sweep us away." —Isaiah 64:6

Our best efforts, measured against God's perfect holiness, fall devastatingly short.

"People ruin their lives by their own foolishness and then are angry at the Lord."—Proverbs 19:3

The Problem: Sin's Separation

Why can't human effort open the door to eternal life? Not because God is cruel or unreasonable. Not because He enjoys watching us struggle. But because the problem isn't our lack of effort—it's sin itself.

"For all have sinned and fall short of the glory of God." —Romans 3:23

Sin has separated us from God.
It's not a matter of degree—as if some people are "close enough" to God's standard while others fall further away.

We've all missed the mark entirely. No amount of human striving can undo this separation.

"For the wages of sin is death, but the gift of God is eternal life in Christ Jesus our Lord." —Romans 6:23

Sin's consequence is death—
Spiritual Separation from God.
No human work can pay this debt.

The Unbridgeable Gap Imagine standing on one side of the Grand Canyon, trying to jump across to the other side. It doesn't matter if you're an Olympic athlete or completely out of shape—the gap is too vast. You could train your entire life and still fall short.

The gap between sinful humanity and Holy God is infinitely wider. Our best attempts to bridge it through good works, religious devotion, or moral living are like trying to build a ladder to the moon.

"For it is by grace you have been saved, through faith—and this is not from yourselves, it is the gift of God—not by works, so that no one can boast."
—Ephesians 2:8-9

If we could earn salvation through our efforts,
it wouldn't be a gift—**it would be a wage.**
We could boast about achieving it.
But God designed salvation differently,
for a very important reason.

Why God Couldn't Accept Our Efforts:
If God accepted our good works as payment for eternal life, several problems would arise:

1. We would never know if we'd done enough. How many good deeds equal eternal life? Where's the finish line?
2. We would boast in our achievement rather than being grateful for God's Grace.
3. Salvation would depend on our strength rather than God's power.
4. Only the privileged would qualify.

Those with more resources, education, or

opportunities would have an advantage. God's way is far better. He doesn't ask us to achieve what we cannot accomplish. **Instead, He offers what only He can provide.**

The Door We Cannot Open:
The door to eternal life exists. God hasn't hidden it or made it impossible to find. But it's a door that cannot be opened from our side, no matter how hard we push, how many keys we try, or how long we work at it. Human effort, no matter how sincere or sustained, can never open the door to heaven.

This isn't cruelty on God's part—it's reality. We need a different way, a door that opens from the other side. And that's exactly what God provided. The door stands locked from our side. Every human key we've tried—good works, religious devotion, moral perfection—has failed. We cannot open it. We cannot earn our way through it. We cannot force it.
But what humanity could never accomplish, **God has done.** Let me show you the Door He opened—and the only way through...

CHAPTER 4
THE DOOR GOD OPENED:
JESUS CHRIST

If human effort cannot open the door to eternal life, how can anyone enter? The answer is both simple and profound: God opened the door Himself by sending His Son, Jesus Christ.

"I am the gate; whoever enters through me will be saved. They will come in and go out, and find pasture."
—John 10:9

Jesus isn't just showing us the door—He is the door. God's Initiative. We couldn't reach God, so God reached down to us. While we were still trapped in sin, separated from Him, God acted.

"But God demonstrates his own love for us in this: While we were still sinners, Christ died for us."—Romans 5:8

God didn't wait for us to clean ourselves up or prove ourselves worthy. He came to us in our broken, sinful state and provided the solution we desperately needed but could never create ourselves.

Jesus: Fully God, Fully Man

For Jesus to be the bridge between God and humanity, He had to be both fully God and fully man. As God, Jesus had the power and authority to forgive sins and grant eternal life. As man, He could represent humanity and pay the price for our sins.

"In the beginning was the Word, and the Word was with God, and the Word was God... The Word became flesh and made his dwelling among us. We have seen his glory, the glory of the one and only Son, who came from the Father, full of grace and truth." —John 1:1, 14

God became one of us so He could save us.

The Cross: Payment for Sin

On the Cross, Jesus accomplished what no human effort could ever achieve.
He paid the debt we owed but couldn't pay.

"For Christ also suffered once for sins, the righteous for the unrighteous, to bring you to God. He was put to death in the body but made alive in the Spirit."
—1 Peter 3:18

The righteous one died for the unrighteous. The sinless one took the punishment for sinners. This wasn't merely a good man dying unjustly—this was God's perfect plan to reconcile humanity to Himself.

"God made him who had no sin to be sin for us, so that in him we might become the righteousness of God."
—2 Corinthians 5:21

Jesus took our sin upon Himself so we could receive **His Righteousness.**
This is the heart of the gospel—

"THE GREATEST TRADE IN HISTORY."

The Resurrection: Victory Over Death
Jesus' death paid for our sins, but His resurrection proved His victory over death itself.

"For what I received I passed on to you as of first importance: that Christ died for our sins according to the Scriptures, that he was buried, that he was raised on the third day according to the Scriptures."—1 Corinthians 15:3-4

Death couldn't hold Jesus. The grave couldn't contain Him. He rose victorious, offering eternal life to all who believe in Him.

The Only Way

Some people find it troubling that Jesus claims to be the only way to God. But this exclusivity isn't arrogance—it's necessity. Only Jesus lived a sinless life. Only Jesus could pay the price for sin. **Only Jesus conquered death.**

"I am the way and the truth and the life. No one comes to the Father except through me." —John 14:6

This isn't narrow-mindedness; **it's the reality of how God chose to save us.** Would we prefer that God left us with no way at all? Or multiple complicated paths where we could never be certain we'd chosen correctly?

“Salvation is found in no one else, for there is no other name under heaven given to mankind by which we must be saved.”—Acts 4:12

Some ask: “But what about people who never heard about Jesus?” This is a compassionate question. Here’s what we know:
God is perfectly just and perfectly loving. He will judge each person fairly based on what they knew and how they responded to it. Our responsibility is not to judge others, but to respond to what God has revealed to us—that—
Jesus is the way, the truth, and the life.

The Open Door:
The door to eternal life now stands open. Jesus opened it through His death and resurrection. It’s not locked. It’s not hidden. It’s not available only to special people or those who meet certain qualifications. **The door is open to anyone who will enter through Jesus.**

“Here I am! I stand at the door and knock. If anyone hears my voice and

opens the door, I will come in and eat with that person, and they with me." —Revelation 3:20

Notice: Jesus is knocking. He's calling.
He's waiting. The door is ready.
The question is: **Will we enter?**

The Door is open. Jesus Christ Himself is that Door. But what lies beyond it? What is this eternal life He offers? The Fountain of Youth—you're about to discover it's been real all along.

"For the Son of Man came to seek and to save the lost." —Luke 19:10

If you knew Jesus —not the people who claim to represent Him, but Jesus Himself— you would run to Him. And so I raise a glass—not of wine, but of wonder. **How blessed am I?** That the God of all creation would pursue a man like me, chase me down through my worst years, and refuse to let me go. And I am very grateful beyond what words can hold.

CHAPTER 5
FATHER, FORGIVE THEM:
THE LAMB OF GOD

The Revelation of Divine Love at the Cross

"Behold! The Lamb of God who takes away the sin of the world!"—John 1:29

At the center of human history stands a moment that does not merely shape history—
"It redeems it."

That moment is the crucifixion of Jesus Christ. This was not merely an execution, nor simply an act of injustice.

It was the unveiling of divine love in its most unrestrained, sacrificial, and forgiving form.

When John the Baptist first saw Jesus,
he did not call Him teacher or prophet.

He declared something far deeper:
"Behold, the Lamb of God."

In those words, the entire mission of Christ was revealed. He came not only to teach— but to be given. And at the cross, that declaration found its complete fulfillment.

THE MOST ASTONISHING WORDS EVER SPOKEN

Imagine the scene. The nails have already been driven through His hands and feet. Roman soldiers kneel at the foot of the cross — not in worship, but casting lots, gambling for the robe that once covered the Son of God. The crowd presses close, faces twisted in mockery. Some shout, "If You are the Son of God, come down from the cross!" Others sneer, "He saved others; He cannot save Himself." Women weep. Disciples have fled.

And the man who made the stars with His spoken word hangs bleeding, stripped, and scorned above them all.

And yet — in the very middle of this brutality — before He cries out in thirst, before He breathes His last — He speaks.

Not in condemnation. Not in rage.

Not in the divine authority that could have called ten thousand angels to His side.

He speaks in intercession.

"Father, forgive them, for they do not know what they are doing."—Luke 23:34

These are not the words of a victim. These are the words of a Savior. On the instrument of His own execution, Jesus becomes the world's greatest intercessor, and the first voice spoken from that cross is the voice of grace.

God's love does not wait for repentance before it extends mercy – it reaches into the darkest expressions of sin and offers forgiveness in advance.

THE COST OF THAT GRACE

Grace is not the dismissal of justice – it is justice fulfilled through sacrifice. Every blow, every drop of blood, every moment of agony bore the full weight of human sin.

Christ was not merely suffering with humanity – **He was suffering for humanity.**

Isaiah foretold it centuries before it happened.

"He was wounded for our transgressions, He was bruised for our

iniquities; the chastisement for our peace was upon Him, and by His stripes we are healed."— Isaiah 53:5

The voices that taunted Him — "If You are the Son of God, come down from the cross!" — reveal a profound misunderstanding of divine power. True power was not displayed by escaping the cross, but by remaining upon it. **Love held Him there.**

The nails did not bind Him — obedience to the Father and compassion for humanity did.

"He was oppressed and afflicted, yet he did not open his mouth; he was led like a lamb to the slaughter, and as a sheep before its shearers is silent, so he did not open his mouth."— Isaiah 53:7

DICE AT THE FOOT OF THE CROSS. Perhaps no image in the Passion narrative is more haunting than the soldiers casting lots for Jesus' clothing. While the Creator of heaven and earth hangs dying above them, men kneel in the dirt gambling for a seamless robe — unaware that the very scene they are acting out was recorded in Scripture a thousand years before they were born.

"They divide my clothes among them and cast lots for my garment."
—Psalm 22:18

It is a picture of human indifference at its starkest — ordinary men doing an ordinary thing, completely blind to the eternal weight of what surrounds them. Even in chaos, God's sovereign plan was unfolding.

The apparent triumph of evil was, in reality, the means by which redemption was being secured. The dice roll. The robe is won. And forgiveness continues to pour from His lips.

HE FORGAVE BEFORE THEY ASKED

Christ's prayer -**"Father, forgive them"** — was not limited to those physically present at Calvary. **It extended across time to all of humanity.** The soldiers did not know they were **crucifying the Lord of glory.**

The crowd did not know **they were rejecting their only hope of salvation.** Even the religious leaders did not recognize in

Jesus the fulfillment of every prophecy they had ever read.

"None of the rulers of this age understood it, for if they had, they would not have crucified the Lord of glory." — 1 Corinthians 2:8

Their ignorance did not slow His forgiveness. He did not wait for understanding, for remorse, or for confession. **He forgave first.**

Sin was judged — fully and completely —
but not upon the sinners themselves.
It was placed upon the sinless Lamb of God.
Nothing is beyond the reach of that cross.

IT IS FINISHED — THE VEIL IS TORN

As Christ breathed His last, He did not whisper in defeat. **He declared in victory — "It is finished."** The Greek word is **Tetelestai** — a single word meaning paid in full, completed, accomplished.

Every prophecy satisfied.
Every debt cancelled.
Every barrier between God and man removed in one final, sovereign act.

"And when Jesus had cried out again in a loud voice, he gave up his spirit. At that moment the curtain of the temple was torn in two from top to bottom. The earth shook, the rocks split." — Matthew 27:50–51

The veil that hung in the Temple was no ordinary curtain. It was sixty feet high and thirty feet wide and four inches thick — the barrier between the Holy Place and the Holy of Holies, the very presence of God. No human hand could tear it. But God tore it — from top to bottom, not from the bottom up.

The tearing of the veil was not a small moment —it was the fulfillment of everything. The prophecy completed in all its fullness.

For generations, only one man —the High Priest —could enter the Holy of Holies, and only once a year, on the Day of Atonement, carrying the blood of a sacrifice.

The common person could never simply walk in. The presence of God was sealed behind that curtain, separated from sinful humanity by law,

ritual, holiness, and judgment.
One wrong step meant death.

But when Christ cried **"It is finished"** and breathed His last, God reached down from heaven and tore that curtain in two —not from the bottom where human hands could reach, **but from the top where only God could.**

At that same moment the earth shook beneath every living foot, and the stones of the Temple trembled as the hand of God tore through it.

Creation itself recoiled at the weight of what just had been accomplished.

In that single act, He declared that the age of distance was over.

No more earthly High Priest standing between you and God. No more annual sacrifice needed. No more barrier between a broken person and a holy God. Every man, every woman, every soul who ever felt too sinful, too far gone, or too forgotten —the way is open.

The cross is the way home. Not because we earned it. **Because the Lamb paid for it.**

The way is open.
The separation is over.
Come in.

The earth shook. The rocks split. The graves opened. Creation itself bore witness to what had just happened. **The Lamb of God had taken away the sin of the world** – and heaven and earth shuddered at the weight of it.

HE STILL INTERCEDES

The prayer He prayed on Calvary was not a single moment in time – it was a declaration of His eternal posture toward broken humanity.

The Lamb who was slain is also risen. He is not an angry God waiting to condemn you. He is the risen Lord who already prayed your forgiveness before you ever knew you needed it.

"Therefore he is able to save completely those who come to God through him, because he always lives to intercede for them." – Hebrews 7:25

The cross is not a monument to human cruelty. **It is the altar of divine love.** The first words spoken from it were not condemnation, but grace —**unearned, undeserved, unstoppable grace** —extended to every man, woman, and child who has ever looked up and finally understood what they were looking at.

If you have lived your life casting dice at the foot of the cross — preoccupied with the small concerns of this world while the greatest love in history was poured out within arm's reach— **know this: the prayer still stands.**

"Father, forgive them."

That word them includes you.
It always has.

Behold the Lamb of God.

The question is not whether He was given.
The question is whether you will receive Him.

CHAPTER 6
HEAVEN: THE TRUE FOUNTAIN OF YOUTH

For thousands of years, humanity has searched for the Fountain of Youth—a mythical source of eternal life and perpetual vitality. Kings funded expeditions. Explorers risked their lives. Scientists pursued formulas. The search continues even today through anti-aging research and life-extension technologies. The Fountain of Youth is not mythical at all. It is real—but it has been misunderstood from the beginning.

Heaven: Eternal Life Itself.

The true Fountain of Youth is Heaven—eternal life in the presence of God. It's not a magical spring that extends our earthly existence. It's our complete transformation into imperishable, eternal life.

"For the perishable must clothe itself with the imperishable, and the mortal with immortality. When the perishable has been clothed with the imperishable, and the mortal with immortality, then

the saying that is written will come true: 'Death has been swallowed up in victory.'"—1 Corinthians 15:53-54

In Heaven, we won't simply live longer—we'll live forever in bodies that never age, never decay, and never die. No More Death, Pain, or Tears. Heaven isn't just an extension of earthly life with its struggles and sorrows continuing indefinitely. It's the complete removal of everything that causes suffering.

"And I heard a loud voice from the throne saying, 'Look! God's dwelling place is now among the people, and he will dwell with them. They will be his people, and God himself will be with them and be their God. He will wipe every tear from their eyes. There will be no more death or mourning or crying or pain, for the old order of things has passed away.'"—Revelation 21:3-4

Imagine a life with no sickness, no aging, no loss, no grief, no fear of death. That's not fantasy—that's God's promise of Heaven.

Perfect Fellowship with God. The greatest treasure of Heaven isn't the absence of suffering—**"It's the presence of God." We'll experience unbroken, perfect fellowship with our Creator.**

No longer will there be any curse. The throne of God and of the Lamb will be in the city.—Revelation 22:3

We'll see God's face. We'll know Him fully.

The longing He placed in our hearts will finally be completely satisfied. **A Real Place.** Heaven isn't a state of mind or a metaphor for inner peace. It's a real place that God has prepared for His children.

"My Father's house has many rooms; if that were not so, would I have told you that I am going there to prepare a place for you? And if I go and prepare a place for you, I will come back and take you to be with me that you also may be where I am." —John 14:2-3

Jesus is preparing a specific place for us.

He's coming back to take us there.
Heaven is our eternal home.

Immortality Already Won.

Here's the most amazing truth:
for those who trust in Jesus, immortality isn't something we're still searching for—
— it's already secured.

"Jesus said to her, 'I am the resurrection and the life. The one who believes in me will live, even though they die; and whoever lives by believing in me will never die. Do you believe this?'"
—John 11:25-26

Through Jesus, death becomes merely a doorway, not an ending. Our physical bodies may die, but we—our true selves—live forever.

The Fountain That Never Runs Dry:

Earthly fountains run dry.
Medical breakthroughs have limitations.
Anti-aging treatments eventually fail.
But the eternal life Jesus offers never ends.

"Jesus answered, 'Everyone who drinks this water will be thirsty again, but

whoever drinks the water I give them will never thirst. Indeed, the water I give them will become in them a spring of water welling up to eternal life.'"
—John 4:13-14

This is the true Fountain of Youth—not a source we must repeatedly return to, but a spring of eternal life welling up within us, never running dry.

Why Search Any Longer?

Humanity has searched for millennia for what **God offers freely in Jesus Christ.**

We've pursued immortality through every means imaginable, yet the answer has been available all along.

Heaven—eternal life in God's presence—is the Fountain of Youth we've been seeking. And access to it isn't earned through expedition or discovery, achievement or payment.

It's received as a gift through Jesus Christ. You've seen the love of the Father who created you. You've felt the longing He placed within you. You've learned why human effort always fails.

You've discovered the Door Jesus opened. You've glimpsed the eternal home that awaits.

Now comes the most important moment of all —the invitation to receive what you could never earn.

CHAPTER 7
AN INVITATION TO RECEIVE, NOT ACHIEVE

We've established several crucial truths:

- God placed a longing for eternity within every human heart.
- Human effort cannot bridge the gap between us and God.
- Jesus opened the door to eternal life through His death and resurrection.
- Heaven is the true Fountain of Youth we've been searching for.

Now comes the most important question: How do we receive this gift of eternal life?

"A Gift, Not a Wage"

Eternal life isn't something we earn—it's something we receive. And sometimes the hardest thing to receive is grace when we feel weak.

When Weakness Becomes the Doorway

There is something in us that quietly resists weakness. We try to repair it, manage it, conceal it, or rise above it. We imagine that if we could just become a little stronger — spiritually steadier, emotionally healthier, morally consistent —then we would finally be ready for God.

Finally useful. Finally acceptable.

But the Apostle Paul learned a gentler truth.

He carried what he called a "thorn in the flesh" — something persistent, something humbling, something that would not leave. Like any sincere believer, he asked God to remove it.

He prayed more than once. He hoped for relief. He trusted that surely God would take it away.

Yet the thorn remained. And instead of an explanation, God gave him a promise:

But he said to me, "My grace is sufficient for you, for My power is made perfect in weakness." Therefore I will boast all the more gladly about my weakness, so that Christ's power may rest on me.
—2 Corinthians 12:9

God did not remove the weakness — He revealed His grace and strength within it.

Pause there.

God did not say His power would be perfected when Paul improved. He did not say it would shine once Paul overcame. He did not say it would arrive after victory.

**He said in our weakness,
His power is made perfect.**

That changes how we see everything. It means the place you feel least adequate may be the very place Christ draws us closest to Him. The burden you have asked Him to lift may become the place where His nearness is most deeply known. Not because suffering is beautiful — **but because grace is.**

Grace does not wait for your strength.
Grace meets you in your need.

Perhaps that is why receiving can feel harder than striving. Striving allows us to maintain control. Receiving asks us to rest. Striving highlights what we can accomplish. Receiving gently shifts the focus to what Christ has already completed. So what if your weakness is not a barrier? **What if it is an opening?**

Paul's response was not bitterness, but freedom. He learned that weakness was not the end of usefulness — **it was the beginning of dependence. And in that dependence, the power of Christ rested upon him.**

That is why, for Christ's sake, I delight in weakness, in insults, in hardship, in persecutions, in difficulties. "For when I am weak, then I am strong."
—2 Corinthians 12:10

The weakness Paul speaks of in one breath is the very weakness he brings to Christ in the next. He is not saying, "Get stronger so Christ can use you." He is saying, "Bring your emptiness—and watch what He fills it with."

Paul was not trusting in his own strength. He was learning to depend completely on Christ. Weakness did not destroy Paul.

It taught him where true strength comes from. The strength Paul discovered was not self confidence—it was complete dependence on Christ.

"I can do all things through Christ who strengthens me." —Philippians 4:13

Not strong in himself. Strong because grace was enough. And if grace was sufficient for Paul, it is also sufficient for you and me.

In the quiet places where you feel smallest, unseen, or unsure — you may discover that you are not being held back at all.

You are being held. God doesn't ask us to achieve salvation; **He asks us to accept it.**

"He saved us, not because of righteous things we had done, but because of His mercy. He saved us through the washing of rebirth and renewal by the Holy Spirit" —Titus 3:5

Think about how gifts work. If someone offers you a gift and you respond by trying to pay for it, you've insulted the giver and missed the point entirely. The appropriate response to a gift is simply to receive it with gratitude.

That's exactly how salvation works.

What God Asks of Us

God's requirements are beautifully simple:

1. BELIEVE

Believe that Jesus is who He claimed to be—the Son of God, the Savior of the world. Believe that His death paid for your sins and His resurrection conquered death.

"For God so loved the world that he gave his one and only Son, that whoever believes in him shall not perish but have eternal life." —John 3:16

2. RECEIVE

Accept Jesus' sacrifice on your behalf. Invite Him into your life as Lord and Savior.

"Yet to all who did receive him, to those who believed in his name, he gave the right to become children of God." — —John 1:12

3. TRUST

Trust that Jesus' work is sufficient. Don't try to add your good works to His finished work. **Rest in what He accomplished.**

"If you declare with your mouth, 'Jesus is Lord,' and believe in your heart that God raised him from the dead, you will be saved." —Romans 10:9

No Complex Formula

Notice what God doesn't require:

- Years of religious training
- Perfect moral behavior
- A certain level of theological understanding
- Membership in a specific church
- Performance of religious rituals
- Making up for past sins

Salvation is accessible to anyone—the educated and uneducated, the young and old, the religious and irreligious.

A child can understand it.
A scholar can't improve upon it.

The Prayer of Invitation. If you're ready to receive God's gift of eternal life, you can tell Him right now. There's no magic formula, but here's a prayer that expresses the heart of faith:

"**Dear God,** I recognize that I'm a sinner and I cannot save myself. I believe that Jesus Christ is Your Son, that He died on the Cross for my sins, and that He rose from the dead. I ask You to forgive my sins. I invite Jesus into my life as my Lord and Savior. Thank You for the gift of eternal life. **In Jesus' name, Amen."**

If you prayed that prayer sincerely, you've just received the greatest gift in existence.

Assurance of Salvation:
How can you know for certain that you have eternal life? Not by feelings or worthiness, but by God's promise.

"And this is the testimony: God has given us eternal life, and this life is in his Son. Whoever has the Son has life; whoever does not have the Son of God does not have life. I write these things to

you who believe in the name of the Son of God so that you may know that you have eternal life."— 1 John 5:11-13

You can know you have eternal life—
not hope so, not think so, but know so—
because God has promised it.

Your First Steps Forward
If you've just prayed to receive Jesus,
Congratulations!

You've begun the greatest adventure of your life. Here are some simple next steps to help you grow:

1. TALK TO GOD DAILY
Prayer is simply talking with God.
Share your thoughts, fears, joys, and questions with Him. He wants to hear from you.

2. READ THE BIBLE
Start with the Gospel of John.
God speaks to us through His Word. Even a few verses a day will help you know Him better.

3. FIND A CHURCH FAMILY

Connect with other believers. We weren't meant to walk this journey alone. Look for a church that teaches the Bible and where you can grow in faith.

4. SHARE YOUR DECISION

Tell someone you trust about your decision to follow Jesus. Sharing what God has done in your heart strengthens your faith and connects you to the encouragement and fellowship of other believers.

5. BE PATIENT WITH YOURSELF

You won't be perfect. Growth takes time. God is patient with you, and you can be patient with yourself.

These are not requirements for salvation—you're already saved!

These are simply ways to grow in your new relationship with God.

The Invitation Remains Open.
God's invitation doesn't expire.

The door Jesus opened remains open. Whether you're reading this at age 5 or 95, whether you've lived a relatively good life or made terrible mistakes, the invitation is the same:

Come.
Believe.
Receive.

"The Spirit and the bride say, 'Come!' And let the one who hears say, 'Come!' Let the one who is thirsty come; and let the one who wishes take the free gift of the water of life." —Revelation 22:17

The Fountain of Youth—
Eternal Life in Heaven— is freely offered.
Will you receive it?

The invitation has been extended.
The choice is yours.

But before you close this book, let me speak directly to your heart one final time about the Father who has been waiting for you all along.

REMEMBER OPPORTUNITIES PASS:

TO LOVE OURSELVES IS TO LOVE GOD.
TO LOVE GOD IS TO LOVE OURSELVES.

A Cry from the Other Side

Jesus Christ gives us one of the most sobering glimpses into eternity in the Gospel of Luke.

He tells of a man who had everything this world could offer—comfort, wealth, and daily satisfaction.

And yet, when his life ended, everything changed. In torment, he cried out:

"Father Abraham, have mercy on me, and send Lazarus, that he may dip the tip of his finger in water, and cool my tongue; for I am tormented in this flame."— Luke 16:24

One drop. Not a river.
Not a cup. Just a drop of water.

The man who once lived in abundance now begs for the smallest relief imaginable— and it is not given.

This is not merely a picture of suffering. It is a revelation of missed opportunity.

The Tragedy of Too Late

What makes this moment so heavy is not just the torment—it is the realization.

While he lived, the rich man had access to everything that truly mattered.

But he did not receive it.

And now, what he once ignored has become what he desperately desires.

"A single drop of water."

"Opportunities pass."

They do not wait forever.

Living Water Is Offered Now

"What the rich man longed for in eternity, is freely offered to us today."

Jesus said,

"Whoever drinks of the water that I shall give him will never thirst." —John 4:14

This is the promise of complete and eternal satisfaction.

**Living water. Not earned.
Not achieved. Given.**

Why Human Effort Fails:
Effort can build a life.
Effort can produce success.
Effort can create the appearance of righteousness.

But effort cannot quench the soul.

Because the soul was not designed to be filled by what man can do, but by what God gives.

To Love God Is to Love Ourselves.
To Love God Is to Love Ourselves Rightly.

Not in pride. Not in self-exaltation.

But in alignment with the One who is life itself.
To love God is to receive His mercy, accept His truth, and drink from what He freely gives.

It is not the elevation of self.
It is the restoration of the self.

The Open Invitation

Right now, while breath is still in your body, you are not asking for a drop.

You are being offered a fountain.

Not later. Not after effort. Now.

The Question Every Heart Must Answer.
Will I continue trying to satisfy this thirst on my own, or will I receive what God is freely offering?

Because one day, the opportunity to choose will pass, and what remains will not be effort or success—**but whether or not we drank.**

As it has been said:
Today, if you hear His voice, do not harden your hearts. —Hebrews 3:15

CHAPTER 8
THE DECISION:
OUR FATHER IS CALLING YOU HOME

The End of the Story—And the Beginning of Yours. This has been the story of God's love for you. Not love as a distant feeling. Not love as a theological concept.

But love as an unchanging pursuit—a Father who has never stopped reaching toward His children, even when they turned away.

For thousands of years, across empires and generations, through silence and revelation, God has been writing one message over and over:

"Come home. I love you. Come home."

He spoke it through prophets.
He demonstrated it through miracles.
He revealed it through Scripture.
And then He entered creation Himself—becoming one of us, walking among us, dying for us—so that the way home would be open forever.

This is not a story that ends with information.
This is a story that ends with invitation.
And the invitation is for you.

Not someday. Not when you are better.
Not when you have figured everything out
or cleaned up your life. **Now.**
Our Father is standing at the door.

He has been standing there all along.
And He is calling your name.

You Don't Need to Be Ready. If you are waiting to feel ready, you will wait forever. If you are waiting to feel worthy, you will never qualify. If you are waiting until you understand everything, you will remain outside indefinitely.

But here is the mercy woven into this moment: God is not asking you to be ready. He is ready. God is not asking you to be worthy. Jesus made you worthy. God is not asking you to understand. **He is asking you to trust.**

The only qualification is willingness.
Are you tired of searching? He sees you.

Are you weary of pretending? He knows you. Are you afraid you have wandered too far? He has been following you the entire time.

"Never will I leave you; never will I forsake you."—Hebrews 13:5

The Father has never left.
The invitation has never been withdrawn.

The gift has never been conditional.
What has changed is not God's posture toward you. What changes now is your response.

This Is What Grace Means

Grace is not a reward for good behavior.
Grace is not a prize for religious performance.
Grace is not something you negotiate, earn, or achieve. Grace is God giving you what you could never deserve, **because He loves you.**

When you come to Jesus Christ,
you are not signing up for a system.
You are entering a relationship.
You are not climbing a ladder. You are walking through a Door that stands wide open.

Therefore, brothers and sisters, since we have confidence to enter the Most Holy Place by the blood of Jesus, by a new and living way opened for us through the curtain, that is, His body, and since we have a great priest over the house of God, let us draw near to God with a sincere heart and with the full assurance that faith brings, having our hearts sprinkled to cleanse us from a guilty conscience and having our bodies washed with pure water.
—Hebrews 10:19-22

Jesus is not demanding. **He is inviting.**
Jesus is not condemning. **He is offering.**
Jesus is not far away. **He is right here — waiting for you to say yes.**

If Your Heart Is Ready, If something inside you is stirring—if you sense that this is the moment you have been moving toward your entire life—then the next step is simple.

You don't need a building.
You don't need a ritual.

You don't need a priest, pastor, or mediator.

You need only to speak honestly to the God who already knows your heart. You can pray in your own words, or you can use one of the prayers below. What matters is not the eloquence of your language. What matters is the sincerity of your heart.
God is not listening for perfection.
He is listening for willingness.

A Simple Prayer of Faith
If you want Simplicity, pray this:
Father, I come to You now, just as I am.
I believe that Jesus Christ is Your Son.
I believe He died for my sins and rose again.
I receive Your gift of eternal life.
Forgive me. Save me. Make me Yours.
Thank You for loving me.
In Jesus' name, Amen.

"Very truly I tell you, whoever hears my word and believes Him who sent me has eternal life and will not be judged but has crossed over from death to life."
—John 5:24

If you prayed that prayer with a sincere heart, you are saved. Not because the words were magic. But because God's promise is true.

You have crossed the threshold.
You are no longer outside.
You are home.

A Longer Prayer of Invitation

If you want to pour out your heart more fully, pray this: Father, I come to You just as I am. Tired from searching. Weary from chasing things that never truly satisfied my heart.
I have looked to the world for meaning, for love, for peace, for life that never fades—and I see now that the world could never give what my soul has always been longing for.

Today, I stop running.

"This is the day the Lord has made;
We will rejoice and be glad in it."
—Psalm 118:24

Today, I admit that I am lost... and that I want to be found. Jesus Christ, I believe You are the Son of God. I believe You came not to condemn me, but to rescue me, forgive me, and make me new. I lay down my pride, my fears, my past, and my confusion. I ask You to forgive me for trusting everything except You.

Wash me clean. Heal what is broken.
Restore my heart and my passion for You,
Lord. I now choose You.

Not the promises of the world. Not temporary pleasure. Not empty fountains that run dry.

Your love that never ages and never fades.
Come into my heart.
I choose the true Fountain of Youth—
Your eternal life, **Your Grace.**
Guide my steps.

Teach me how to live in truth and humility.
Let Your Spirit fill the empty places in me with peace, hope, and quiet strength.
From this moment forward, I trust my eternal future to You. I receive Your gift of life—not earned, not deserved, but freely given through love. Thank You for finding me when I could not find myself. I am Yours. Now and forever.
In Jesus' name, Amen.

If You Already Decided to Follow Jesus
Perhaps you prayed to receive Jesus months or years ago, but somewhere along the way you drifted. Life got busy, doubts crept in, or you simply stopped walking closely with Him.

If that's you, pray this prayer of recommitment:
Father, I once said yes to You, but I have wandered. I got distracted. I doubted. I stopped seeking You the way I once did. But **today,**
I return. Not because I've earned my way back, but because Your love never left. I recommit my life to You. I choose to follow Jesus—not perfectly, but sincerely. Renew my passion for You. Rebuild what I let fall into neglect.
Thank You for never giving up on me.
Thank You for always keeping the door open.
I am home again. **In Jesus' name, Amen.**

You Are Home
If you prayed any of those prayers—even with doubt, even with trembling faith, even with questions still lingering—you have crossed the threshold. You are no longer searching.
You are found.

Our Father is not checking your credentials. He is not evaluating your performance. He is not measuring your worthiness. He is rejoicing.

"In the same way, I tell you, there is rejoicing in the presence of the angels of God over one sinner who repents." —Luke 15:10

Heaven is celebrating you. Not because you are perfect, but because you are loved.

Nothing Can Separate You Now.

You may still have questions.
You may still feel unworthy.
You may still wonder if this is real.
But hear this truth and let it settle deep into your heart:

"For I am convinced that neither death nor life, neither angels nor demons, neither the present nor the future, nor any powers, neither height nor depth, nor anything else in all creation, will be able to separate us from the love of God that is in Christ Jesus our Lord." —Romans 8:38-39

Nothing in your past disqualifies you.
Nothing in your present excludes you.
Nothing in your future can undo what God has done.

The door remains open because God's love does not give up. And you—beloved child—you are home.

The Fountain of Youth Flows Now

This is what humanity has searched for across thousands of years.

Not a myth. Not a legend. Not a dream.

But a real, living relationship with the God who made you, knows you, and will never let you go. The Fountain of Youth is not a place you travel to. **It is a Person you receive.**

Jesus Christ is the source of eternal life.
And eternal life is not merely existence without end—it is knowing God and being known by Him, now and forever.

"Now this is eternal life: that they know you, the only true God, and Jesus Christ, whom you have sent." —John 17:3

Peace now. Rest now. Home forever.

Welcome Home, Beloved
The search is over. The striving can cease.
The weight can be set down. You were created for this—to know God, to be known by Him,
to walk with Him, to rest in Him.
And now, through Jesus Christ, you do.

The love story that began before time—
the story of a Father pursuing His children
with endless patience and unfailing love—
has reached you. And it does not end.

It continues—now and forever—with you in the arms of the One who made you, redeemed you, and will never let you go. **Welcome home.**

"For God did not send his Son into the world to condemn the world, but to save the world through him." —John 3:17

THE FOUNTAIN OF YOUTH - GUARANTEED GRACE = IS HEAVEN

JOHN 3:16-17

The heavens remain perfectly ordered.
The invitation remains open.
Our Father is waiting.
Come home.

THE GREAT COMMISSION

"Feed My sheep."

**He said to him the third time,
Simon Peter, do you love Me?**

**Peter was grieved because
Jesus said to him the third time,
"Do you love Me?"**

And he said to Him,

**"Lord, You know all things;
You know that I love You."**

Jesus said to him,

"Feed My sheep." —John 21:17

NOTES

NOTES

NOTES

www.ingramcontent.com/pod-product-compliance
Lightning Source LLC
LaVergne TN
LVHW090532110826
845146LV00003B/1068